A Step-by-Step Guide

How to Fall

The Basics of Break Falling

Simple basic techniques used in the martial arts of Judo and Jujitsu

Knowing how to fall can protect your limbs.
Knowing how to fall can protect your hips.
Knowing how to fall can protect your neck.
Knowing how to fall can protect your spine.
Knowing how to fall can protect your brain.
Knowing how to fall can save your life!

By D. R Gordon   *2017* © All Rights Reserved

How to Fall

The Basics of Falling

This is a basic informational book about how to safely fall to the ground and in that if this shall happen you may have it in thoughts to protect yourself. Learning to fall properly and safely can be a big step towards facing accidents and also transfer and become a big part for some of the other more difficult lessons that come with intense Judo or Jujitsu training.

Recommendation : Please do not do any of these break falls unless you have seen a doctor or specialist making sure it is ok for you to do any of these techniques. Go slow, take your time and do it right.

Break falling works by using forces and the laws of simple physics

This step-by-step, approach to safe falling sets the stage for developing confidence, coordination, and control. In addition, this method of learning will immediately transfer well to the study of your first throws. The traditional order of learning how to fall, and training your body, is to move from the simple to the more difficult. There are several types of falls. However the five basic types of falls will be discussed with this manual.

With these falling techniques you spread the impact of a fall over the widest area possible you disperse that force over that area. By learning how to place your body correctly and thereby learning to relax as you fall you disperse the force thus reducing the chance of injury. You can practice, and train yourself, on Judo mats, wrestling mats, gymnastic mats and for a more practical use you even practice falling on grass, dirt, tile floors, wood floors and even cement.

Dedication: *To my children hoping they'll never fall and when they do fall will always get up and keep trying again. Love, Dad*

The Basics of Falling

There are seven basic types of Break Falls

- Break Falls. on Back, Squatting and Standing
- Side Break Falls. Side, Squatting, Standing
- Front Break Falls. Front, Squatting, Standing
- Forward Roll Break Fall
- Rear Roll Break Fall
- Spin Out Roll
- Air Roll Break Fall

Everyone should progress at own speeds

Preventing injury and minimize the pain when you fall or is thrown. Fall breaking includes front ways, backwards, right side, and left side break falls and forward roll break fall. In addition to being a basic component of throwing techniques, fall breaking or Ukemi is also a fundamental part of all Judo and Jujitsu techniques. Begin gently and from low postures and gradually perform to faster, higher posture falling and during actual movement of body.

Keep your head tucked or touching chest; and limbs close to body. Hand slaps strike the mat at 45 degree angles no further. Leg should be slightly apart to keep from knocking knees and leg bones.

At first, practice falling from a lying down or low position and gradually move to higher, eventually standing and moving to the fall. Learn one direction of falling, and then learn to in other direction. Fall in standing in place, then add movement as you progress. In the beginning move slowly, carefully and then increase speed over time.

The Basic Arm Palm Hand Technique

The Arm Palm Hand slap consist of part arm, palm and part side hand

This is not a "break fall" however it is part of all falls. The hand should be slightly cupped and the meat side to the hand is the part that touches the floor first including the meat part of your forearm that is used in combination absorbing the forces of the fall.

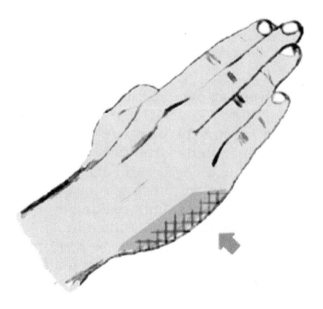

Backward Break Fall - Ushiro Ukemi

Begin with the both arms extended forward at shoulder height and go into to a crouching posture and begin to fall by rolling backwards onto your rounded back with both arms slapping on the floor, preventing an impact shock to the head by raising the head forward, touching chin to chest and looking towards your feet.

Step By Step

From a Laying Back Position

Lay on back looking upward, legs slightly apart. Cross arms across chest, arms slightly bent, hands toward body. Lift head and put chin to chest and looking between your legs. Uncrossing arms at almost 90 degree angles from body lightly slap both hands at same time to floor as you imagine absorbing the shock energy from a fall. While you slap you slightly raise and continue keeping head to chest. Return to back to a lying position with arms crossed, and return head to floor.

From a Sitting Position

Squat by bending knees at 90 degree angles.

Step back with one foot, rock backwards with a slightly curved back. Place chin tucked to chest.= Quickly cross arms slightly across chest, bent, hands toward body

Uncrossing arms at almost 90 degree angles from body lightly slap both hands at same time to floor as you imagine absorbing the shock energy from a fall.

While you slap you slightly raise and continue keeping head to chest.

Return to back to a sitting position with arms crossed and return head relaxed.

From a Standing Position

From a standing position lower body and slightly squat by bending knees.

Placing chin tucked to chest, step back with one foot, lower body, rock backwards with a slightly curved back. Quickly cross arms slightly across chest, bent, hands toward body.

As your back starts to touch slap the mat with both hands 90 degree angles. While you slap you slightly raise and continue keeping head to chest.

Return to back to a sitting position with arms crossed and return head relaxed. Lift hands outward, and with quick motion returning to a standing position.

Sideways Break Fall - Yoko Ukemi

Similar to a back break fall, except hit the mat only with one hand. Put one foot out in front (right foot for a right fall and left for a left fall). With this fall it is important that fall with their legs partially apart as it can be rather painful for your legs and knees to slap together.

Step By Step

From a Lay Back Position

Lay on back looking upward. Turning body to left side or right side, place the one arm further from ground up in the air as if you've been thrown sideways. Lift head and put chin to chest at slight angle face away from floor. Take the other arm, closes to floor, lift slightly bent with hand toward body. Lightly slap the floor arm at a 45 degree angle at same time lifting both legs slightly off ground and placing back to floor separated with the sides of feet touching the floor. Continue keeping head to chest. Return to lying position.

From a Sitting Position

Sit on floor with hands outward and facing towards each other. Placing chin tucked to chest, rock backwards onto back while kicking out the leg same as slap hand side - the floor side. Lean body to left side or right side, place the one arm further from ground up in air as if you been thrown sideways or fell to the side.

As the side of your back starts to touch slap the floor with hand arm at a 45 degree angle. Lift both legs slightly off ground and place back to floor separated and lightly lying with the sides of feet only touching. Lift head and put chin to chest at slight angle face away from floor. Lightly slap the floor arm at a 45 degree angle.

Continue keeping head to chest. Lift hands outward, and with quick motion return to a standing position. Repeat other side

From a Keeling Position

Lean body to left side or right side, place the one arm further from ground up in air as if you've been thrown sideways or fell to the side. Step out either the left or the right leg towards the opposite side of your body.

The same arm and hand on same as leg extending moves outward and prepares to slap the floor. Place the other one arm from ground up in air as if you've been thrown sideways. The slapping arm slightly bent, hand toward body begins to slap the floor. Lift both legs slightly off ground and place back to floor separated and lightly lying with the sides of feet only touching.

Lift head and put chin to chest at slight angle face away from floor. Lightly slap the floor arm at a 45 degree angle.

Continue keeping head to chest. Return to lying position with arms ready and head to mat. Repeat other side.

From a Standing Position

Lean body to left side or right side, place the one arm further from ground up in air as if you were thrown sideways or fell to the side.

Step out either the left or the right leg towards the opposite side of your body.

Kick your left leg toward right foot or right toward left foot.

Proceed to fall to the same side as kicked leg.

The same arm and hand on same as leg that is extending moves outward. Prepare to slap the floor with same arm as kicked leg.

Place the other one arm up in air as if you fell sideways, creating an anti force.

The slapping arm slightly bent, hand toward body begins to slap the floor.

Lift both legs slightly off ground and place back to floor separated and lightly lying with the sides of feet only touching.

Lift head and put chin to chest at slight angle face away from floor. Lightly slap the floor arm at a 45 degree angle. Continue keeping head to chest.

Return to lying position with arms ready and head to mat. Repeat other side.

Front Break Fall - Mae Ukemi

Falling forward with the body extended, striking the floor with both hands and forearms to dissipate the impact.

Step By Step

From Laying on Front Position

Lay on Stomach slightly lift the stomach off ground. Slap the floor lightly with the meat part of hands and forearms at the same time. Turn head to avoid hitting nose and face. Return to a kneeling or a standing position with arms to the sides. Once you reach a point where you can execute a proper kneeling fall then you are ready for a standing forward break fall.

From a Keeling Position

From a kneeling position fall forward and land on front not touching the stomach. Land on the front of body not touching the stomach but landing on the meat part of hands and forearms at the same time as you slap the floor lightly. Turn head to avoid hitting nose and face. Return to a kneeling or a standing position arm to the sides. Once you reach a point where you can execute a proper kneeling fall then you are ready for a standing forward break fall.

From a Standing Position

From a standing position fall forward (can bend knees until confident) and land on front not touching the stomach. Landing on the front of body not touching the stomach but land with the meat part of hands and forearms at the same time as you slap the floor lightly. Turn head to avoid hitting nose and face. Return to a kneeling or a standing position with arm to the sides.

A forward roll is basically a forward somersault roll and a shoulder roll combined, where you avoid touching your head on the mat by tucking and slightly turning the head. The rolling action differs from gymnastics in that the impact is taken across the shoulders by slightly turning the body and using legs as part of impact.

Bring both hands and the right feet forward simultaneously, push strongly forward from both feet and tuck the right arm inward when entering the roll. Strike the mat with the left hand as the feet make contact with the mat.

Forward Roll Break Fall – Mae Mawari Ukemi

Step By Step

From a standing position lower body by stepping forward with one foot. Placing chin tucked to chest, touching both hands to floor in front of you with the same hand that is the same side of the forward foot slightly ahead of the other hand. As you begin to roll forward onto the ground concentrate on the forward hand and arm touching all of the floor and as the shoulder begins to touch, prepare the other hand to slap.

Continue keeping head to chest as you begin the roll. Legs slightly apart the sides should touch the floor as you roll through. Slapping mat you and rolling you should be able to begin standing. Lift hands outward, and with quick motion returning to a standing position.

Spinning Out Roll, Break Fall - Yoko Nage Ukemi

A spin out roll consist of twisting your body while falling towards floor. Slapping with both hands onto floor.

From a Kneeling Position

From a kneeling position begin to twist body and look backwards as you fall. Land on the front of body not touching the stomach. Land on the meat part of hands, forearms and elbows all at the same time as you slap the floor lightly. Turn head to avoid hitting nose and face. Return to a standing position with arms to the sides.

From a Standing Position

From a kneeling position begin to twist body and look backwards as you fall. Land on the front of body not touching the stomach. Land on the meat part of hands, forearms and elbows all at the same time as you slap the floor lightly. Turn head to avoid hitting nose and face. Return to a standing position with arms to the sides.

Rear Roll, Backward Break Fall Ushiro Ukemi

Begin with the both arms extended forward at shoulder height. Go into a crouching posture and fall backwards onto your rounded back with both arms on the mat. To prevent impact shocks to the head at this time, raise the head forward as if looking at your belt.

From Laying on Front Position

Lay on back and lift the legs off floor. Slap the floor lightly with the meat part of hands and forearms at the same time. Turn head to left or right. Roll backwards and stand up

From a Kneeling Position

From a kneeling position, prepare to roll backwards.

Sitting downward and laying to back. Slap the floor lightly with the meat part of hands and forearms at the same time. Turn head to left or right. Roll backwards and stand up.

From a Standing Position

From a standing position, prepare to roll backwards by kneeling. Sitting downward and laying to back. Slap the floor lightly with the meat part of hands and forearms at the same time. Turn head to left or right. Roll backwards and stand up.

Air Roll, Break Fall - Ukemi

An Air Roll consists of whipping your body, falling towards floor, landing sideways while slapping the floor. This is a difficult fall, be careful not to knock your knees or over bend your legs. Go slow and then progress.

Step By Step

From a Standing Position

As your right, or left hand, comes around in a whipping motion, step forward with your foot. As you swing your right - or left hand - down and around the opposite leg whips straight up toward the ceiling. Your body turns in the air prepare to land sideways and slap the mat keeping other hand on your stomach. Stand up.

GLOSSARY   Japanese to English

Ai-yotsu   Same grip used by both persons

Ashi   Foot, leg

Ashi Waza   Foot techniques

Atemi Waza   Striking techniques

Ayumi Ashi   Ordinary pattern of walking

Batsugun   Instant promotion

Budo   Martial ways

Bujutsu   Martial arts

Bushido   Way of the warrior

Chui   Penalty (no longer used)

Dan   Black belt rank

Debana   Opportunity to break balance

Dojo   School or Training hall

Eri   Collar, Lapel

Fudoshin   Immovable spirit

Fusegi   Escapes

Fusen Gachi   Win by default

Goshin Jutsu   Art of self defense

Hajime   Begin

Hando no Kuzushi	Unbalancing by reaction
Hansoku-make disqualification	Most serious penalty,
Hantei	Referee call for judge's decision
Happo no Kuzushi	Kuzushi in 8 directions
Hara	Stomach
Hidari	Left
Hiji	Elbow
Hiki-wake	No decision (tie or draw)
Hikite a sleeve	Pulling hand, usually the hand gripping
Hiza	Knee
Ippon	Victory in one move, one point
Jigotai	Defensive posture
Jikan	Referee call to stop the clock
Jita Kyoei	Principle of mutual prosperity
Joseki	Place of honor, upper seat
Judo	Gentle or flexible way
Judogi	Judo practice uniform
Judoka	One who studies Judo
Ju no Kata	Forms of gentleness
Ju no Ri	Principle of flexibility or yielding

Jujutsu Gentle art

Kaeshi Waza   Counter techniques

Kake   Completion or execution of technique

Kansetsu Waza   Joint locking techniques

Kappo   Resuscitation techniques

Kata   Forms

Kata   Shoulder

Katame no kata   Forms of grappling

Katsu   Resuscitation

Keikoku   Penalty (no longer used)

Kenka Yotsu   Opposite grips used by each person, one
right/one left

Kiai   To gather spirit with a shout

Kime no Kata Forms of decision

Kinshi Waza   Techniques prohibited in competition

Ki o tsuke   Attention

Kodansha   High ranking judoka -- 5th dan and
above

Kodokan   Judo institute in Tokyo where Judo was
founded

Kogeki Seyo   Order for judoka to attack

Koka   Scores less than a yuko

Koshi	Hip
Koshi Waza	Hip techniques
Kubi	Neck
Kumikata	Gripping methods
Kuzure	Modified hold
Kuzushi	Unbalancing the opponent
Kyoshi	Instructor
Kyu	Student rank
Maai	Space or engagement distance
Mae	Forward, front
Mae Sabaki	Frontal escape
Mae Ukemi	Falling forward
Masutemi Waza	Back sacrifice throws
Mate	Stop (wait)
Migi	Right
Mudansha	Students below black belt rank
Mune	Chest
Nage	Throw
Nage no Kata	Forms of throwing
Nagekomi	Repetitive throwing practice
Nage Waza	Throwing techniques

Ne Waza	Techniques on the ground
Obi	Judo belt
Okuden	Secret teachings
Osaekomi	Pin, referee call to begin timing
Osaekomi Waza	Pinning techniques
Osaekomi Toketa	Escape, stop timing of hold
Randori	Free practice
Randori no Kata	Forms of free practice techniques
Randori Waza	Techniques for free practice
Rei	Bow
Reiho	Forms of respect, manners, etiquette
Renraku Waza	Combination techniques
Ritsurei	Standing bow
Seika Tanden	A point in the abdomen that is the center of gravity
Seiryoku Zenyo	Principle of maximum efficiency
Seiza	Formal kneeling posture
Sen	Attack initiative
Sensei	Teacher, instructor
Shiai	Contest
Shiaijo	Competition area

Shido	Penalty, equal to koka score
Shihan	Title for a model teacher or "teacher who sets the standard"
Shime Waza	Choking techniques
Shinpan	Referee
Shintai	Moving forwards, sideways & backwards
Shisei	Posture
Shizentai	Natural posture
Shomen	Dojo front
Sode	Sleeve
Soke	Founder of a martial art or ryu
Sono Mama	Stop action; command to freeze
Sore Made	Finished, time is up
Sute Geiko	Randori throwing practice against a higher level judoka
Sutemi Waza	Sacrifice techniques
Tachi Waza	Standing techniques
Tai Sabaki	Body control, turning
Tatami	Mat
Te	Hand, arm
Te Waza	Hand techniques
Tekubi	Wrist

Tokui Waza	Favorite or best technique
Tori	Person performing a technique
Tsugi Ashi	Walking by bringing one foot up to another
Tsukuri	Entry into a technique, positioning
Tsurite	Lifting hand
Uchikomi	Practice without completion
Ude	Arm
Uke	Person receiving the technique
Ukemi	Breakfall techniques
Ushiro	Backward, rear
Ushiro Sabaki	Back movement control
Ushiro Ukemi	Falling backward
Waki	Armpit
Waza	Technique
Waza Ari	Near ippon or half point
Yoko	Side
Yoko Kaiten Ukemi	Sideways rolling break fall
Yoko Sutemi Waza	Side sacrifice throws
Yoko Ukemi	Falling sideways
Yoshi	Resume action, continue

Yubi	Finger
Yudansha	Person who earned the black belt
Yudanshakai	Black belt association
Yuko	Score less than a waza-ari
Yusei Gachi	Win by judge's decision
Zanshin	Awareness
Zarei	Kneeling salutation
Zenpo Kaiten Ukemi	Forward rolling break fall

Zanshin Numbers

1 – Ichi	2 – Ni	3 – San	4 – Shi
5 – Go	6 – Roku	7 – Shichi	8 – Hachi
9 – Ku	10 – Ju	11 - Juichi (10 plus one)	

12 - Juni (10 plus 2)

19 - Juku (10 plus 9)   20 - Niju (2 10's)

29 - Nijuku (2 10's plus a 9)

30 - Sanju (3 10's)   35 - Sanjugo (3 10's plus a 5)

99 - Kujuku (9 10's plus a 9)

100 – Hyaku	1000 – Sen	10,000 - Man
100,000 – Juman	1,000,000 - Hyakuman	
10,000,000 – Senman	100,000,000 - Oku	

A Step-by-Step Guide

How to Fall

The Basics of Break Falling

Simple basic techniques used in the martial arts of Judo and Jujitsu

By D. R. Gordon

ISBN: *9781521320372*
Imprint: Independently published

Printed in Great Britain
by Amazon

15078304R00020